# TECHNOLOGY IN THE
# ANCIENT AMERICAS

CHARLIE SAMUELS

Gareth Stevens
Publishing

Please visit our website, www.garethstevens.com. For a free color catalog of all our high-quality books, call toll-free 1-800-542-2595 or fax 1-877-542-2596.

Library of Congress Cataloging-in-Publication Data

Samuels, Charlie.
Technology in the ancient Americas / by Charlie Samuels.
 p. cm. — (Technology in the ancient world)
Includes index.
ISBN 978-1-4339-9621-4 (pbk.)
ISBN 978-1-4339-9622-1 (6-pack)
ISBN 978-1-4339-9620-7 (library binding)
1. Technology—Mexico—History—Juvenile literature. 2. Technology—Central America—History—Juvenile literature. 3. Aztecs—History—juvenile literature. 4. Mayas—History—Juvenile literature. 5. Incas—History—Juvenile literature. I. Samuels, Charlie, 1961-. II. Title.
F1219.S25 2014
970—dc23

Published in 2014 by
Gareth Stevens Publishing
111 East 14th Street, Suite 349
New York, NY 10003

© 2014 Brown Bear Books Ltd

For Brown Bear Books Ltd:
Editorial Director: Lindsey Lowe
Managing Editor: Tim Cooke
Children's Publisher: Anne O'Daly
Art Director: Jeni Child
Designer: Lynne Lennon
Picture Manager: Sophie Mortimer

**Picture Credits**
**Front Cover: Thinkstock:** istockphoto

**Alamy:** Mireille Vautier 32; **Bridgeman Art Library:** 38, 39; **Corbis:** Richard A. Cooke 12, Charles & Josette Lenars 20; **Getty Images:** DEA/Gianni Dagli Orti 41, Werner Forman/UIG 35; **istockphoto:** 18, 33; **Library of Congress:** 5; **Public Domain:** 34, Walters Art Museum 42; **Shutterstock:** 31, 36, Paulo Afonso 6, Fraencesco Dazzi 1, 24, Herbert Eisengruber 37, Amy Nichole Harris 29, Pablo Hidalgo 25, Irafael 30, Kenneth Keifer 17, Tomaz Kunst 22, Joel Shawn 11; **Thinkstock:** istockphoto 7, 9, 10, 14, 16, 26, 28, 40, Top Photo Group 4.

All other artworks © Brown Bear Books Ltd

Brown Bear Books has made every attempt to contact the copyright holder. If you have any information please contact smortimer@windmillbooks.co.uk

Manufactured in the United States of America

CPSIA compliance information: Batch #CS13GS. For further information contact Gareth Stevens, New York, New York at 1-800-542-2595.

# CONTENTS

# INTRODUCTION

Centuries before Europeans arrived in the Americas, native peoples were outstanding builders. When the first Spaniards arrived early in the 16th century, they were astonished at the cities of the Aztec and Inca. Many early American cultures did not build in stone and many lived nomadic lives. They left few records. But in the deserts of what is now the U.S. Southwest, in the jungles of Mesoamerica (southern Mexico and Central America), and in the Andes

The Maya built this tomb for King Pakal in the city of Palenque in southern Mexico during the seventh century C.E.

The Spaniards were shocked by Aztec human sacrifice. Victims were killed on top of high pyramids and their bodies thrown off.

Mountains, people achieved high levels of craftsmanship. Innovation helped them adapt to what were often hostile environments. Technology gradually changed in a series of tiny improvements, rather than in great steps.

## THREE MIGHTY EMPIRES

This book covers a period from about 1000 B.C.E. to about 1550 C.E. It concentrates on the empires of the Maya and Aztec of Mexico, and the Inca of Peru. The Maya Empire declined by the 10th century C.E. The later empires of the Aztec and Inca lasted until the Spaniards arrived in Mexico in 1517 and in Peru in 1532. Weakened by political division and facing gunpowder weapons, the empires fell. This book will introduce you to examples of the remarkable technology used in the Americas before the Europeans arrived.

# TECHNOLOGICAL BACKGROUND

Compared with other ancient civilizations, those of the Americas began relatively late. But before the great Aztec and Inca empires arose in the 15th and 16th centuries, other civilizations had achieved high levels of technological accomplishment. They included the Maya, whose culture began as early as 1500 B.C.E. It had largely vanished by the middle of the ninth century C.E. The Aztec and Inca drew on the technology of these earlier peoples. The Aztec, for example, adapted the Mayan calendar and forms of Mayan writing.

The Olmec carved huge heads in rock. The heads may represent people who played a sacred ball game.

The pyramids of Teotihuacán in Mexico date from the first century C.E. Over 1,400 years later, the Aztec believed they had been built by the gods.

## OLMEC, TOLTEC, AND MOCHE

The Olmec of Mexico (1200 B.C.E.–400 C.E.) built large earth mounds to serve as ceremonial centers. They transported huge boulders without any wheeled transport, probably by using rafts on lakes and rivers. Later peoples built stone pyramids instead of mounds. The Toltec (c.900–1200 C.E.) built their capital city of Tula in central Mexico around a stepped temple pyramid. They also built huge basalt statues, known as Chac Mools. The Moche of Peru flourished between the second and eighth centuries. They grew crops and built canals to irrigate them. They traveled in reed boats. Such technology was also used later by the Aztec and Inca.

# FARMING

Life in Mesoamerica was based on farming. By the time the Spaniards arrived, the Mesoamericans were some of the most advanced farmers anywhere. They grew food plants that were later introduced to the rest of the world, such as the potato. Corn was the most important crop. It was used as food and to make beer.

## Harvesting corn

Woolen papoose for baby

Early corn cobs were only 1 inch (2.5 cm) long (left). It took 5,000 years of farming, for the modern cob to appear.

Stone-bladed ax to harvest crops

The American peoples bred many different varieties of corn, which grew even at high altitudes in the Andes.

How people farmed depended on where they lived. In the highlands, the Inca used terracing to farm on the steep mountainsides. In the Mexican lowlands, the Aztec reclaimed land from swamps and lakes by making chinampas. These were built up beds of fertile earth on top of a base of reeds. They planted seeds using a digging stick, or *uictli*.

## MAYA FARMING

The Maya built drainage canals in the Yucatán and made raised beds like the Aztec chinampas. They turned the soil with digging sticks and stone-bladed hoes. They planted corn (maize) on the ridges in the soil, with beans and squash in the furrows in between.

## TECHNICAL SPECS

- None of the Mesoamerican cultures used plows. Farmers turned the soil with digging sticks made from strong wood.
- The Aztec had no draft animals. They relied on human labor.
- The Maya learned to boil corn with lime or ground-up snail shells; otherwise a chemical in the corn would cause niacin deficiency.
- The Inca preserved potatoes by freezing them. They left the potatoes out overnight in the cold mountains. During the day, when the potatoes thawed, they walked on them to squeeze out moisture. After a few days, the potatoes (or chuño) were ready to be stored for up to a year.

# TERRACES AND IRRIGATION

These narrow terraces were built by the Inca at the city of Machu Picchu, high in the Andes Mountains.

For the Inca who lived high up in the Andes, the soil was poor and the ground was too steep to grow crops. To solve the problem, the Inca built flat terraces on the steep mountainsides. The Inca and other American peoples also built canals for irrigation.

As well as creating more land for crops, the terraces helped prevent erosion of the soil by wind or rain. The Inca dug narrow steps into the mountainside. The steps were supported with stone walls.

## CANAL BUILDING

To irrigate the terraces, the Inca built canals along the contours of the slopes. In North America, the Hohokam of the Sonoran Desert (c.200–1400 C.E.) built canals to irrigate their fields. They used weirs to control the flow of the water from the Gila River.

## TECHNICAL SPECS

- At the peak of the Inca Empire in the 16th century C.E., terraces covered 3,860 square miles (10,000 sq km).
- The stone retaining walls helped keep the soil warm during cold nights. This helped extend the growing season.
- Inca terraces conserved water well. The soil stayed damp for six months after rain.
- The Inca mixed the soil with small stones; otherwise the soil would have expanded after rain and pushed out the retaining wall.
- The Inca made mortar to build canals from a mixture of cement, lime, sand, and water.

The Inca diverted rivers such as the Urubamba to water fields in the few flat-floored valleys.

# MOUND BUILDING

By 1000 B.C.E., parts of North America were settled by farming peoples. They still gathered wild plants, but they also grew crops. Some built huge earthworks, probably as tombs or for ceremonial purposes. Mound building continued for about 2,000 years. As many as 10,000 people lived in the settlement of Cahokia, in present-day Illinois.

Serpent Mound may have had an astrological purpose. It seems to align with the position of the sun on important days of the year.

At its peak, around 1100 C.E., Cahokia had more than 100 mounds. The largest is Monk's Mound, a flat-topped structure with four terraces.

## SERPENT MOUND

In what is now Ohio, natives built a mound around 1070 C.E. in the shape of a long serpent following the curves of the land. It may have had an astronomical meaning. Its coils align with the equinoxes and solstices. At Emerald Mound in Mississippi, the Natchez people flattened a hill to make a large platform.

## TECHNICAL SPECS

- The mound builders had no carts or pack animals. They had to carry the earth in baskets.
- Monk's Mound at Cahokia contains about 780,000 cubic yards (600,000 cu m) of earth.
- On the platform on top of Emerald Mound stood two flat-topped earth pyramids. The larger was almost 33 feet (10 m) tall.
- If the Serpent Mound was built in 1070 C.E., it may have marked two astronomical events: the explosion of a supernova in 1054 and the coming of Halley's Comet in 1066.

## Cahokia

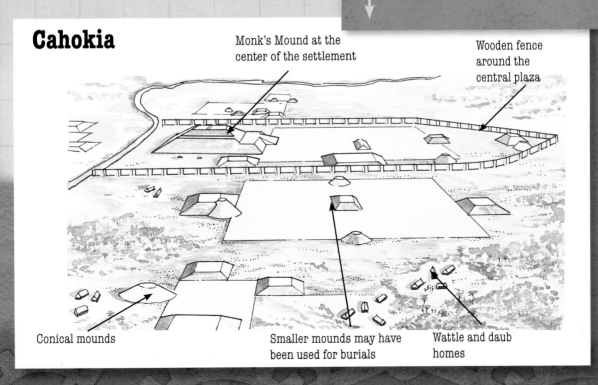

Monk's Mound at the center of the settlement

Wooden fence around the central plaza

Conical mounds

Smaller mounds may have been used for burials

Wattle and daub homes

# PYRAMIDS AND ZIGGURATS

Thousands of years after the Egyptians built their famous pyramids, Mesoamerican peoples built stepped pyramids, or ziggurats. The pyramids all had a religious purpose, but they are not related. The two cultures came up with the same solution to the problem of building tall structures.

The Maya built this pyramid at Chichén Itzá between the 9th and 12th centuries C.E. in honor of the god Kukulkán.

## Teotihuacán

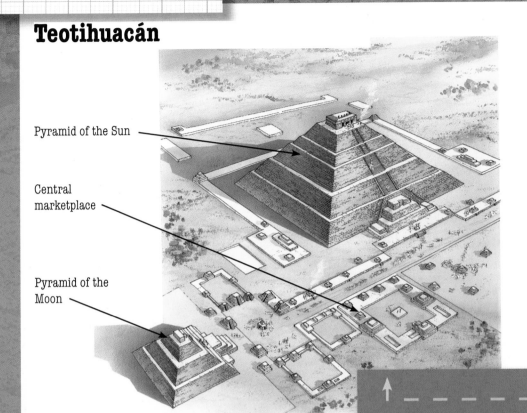

Pyramid of the Sun

Central marketplace

Pyramid of the Moon

## SERIES OF PYRAMIDS

The Olmec built the earliest pyramid in the Americas in about 900 B.C.E. at La Venta. Later, the Maya built pyramids from stone blocks with steep steps. The pyramids had temples at the top. In Teotihuacán, in Mexico, the Pyramid of the Sun and the Pyramid of the Moon were built in the first century C.E. They stood on an avenue lined by smaller pyramids. The Aztec built pyramids in the heart of their capital, Tenochtitlán. Priests used altars on top of the pyramids to sacrifice prisoners to the gods.

## TECHNICAL SPECS

- Olmec pyramids represented the sacred mountain the Olmec believed reached up to heaven.
- The Maya city of Tikal had six tall pyramids, each with a temple on top.
- Mayan pyramids represented the three levels of the Maya universe: the underworld, the earthly world, and the heavenly world.
- At Teotihuacán, human sacrifices were buried in the foundations of the Pyramid of the Moon.
- The Pyramid of the Sun at Teotihuacán was 210 feet (64 m) tall; its base measured 720 by 760 feet (220 by 232 m).

# CLIFF HOUSES

Beneath a cliff in Canyon de Chelly, Arizona, the White House was home to a whole Anasazi community.

In the Southwest of North America, the nomadic Anasazi settled in communities around the sixth century C.E. Corn changed the Anasazi's way of life. The Anasazi settled in the region now known as the Four Corners, where Colorado, Arizona, New Mexico, and Utah meet. They built their homes high up on cliffs for protection.

The early Anasazi lived in homes made from adobe, or mud brick. Some were partly dug into the ground. By the 13th century C.E., they lived in stone houses up to four stories high. The houses had no windows or doors on the ground floor. Ladders led to entrances in the roof.

## HOMES ON CLIFFS

At Mesa Verde, the Anasazi built homes in shallow caves and overhangs in cliff faces. The houses were accessed by ladders. The builders had no metal tools. They shaped sandstone blocks for building by chipping them with harder stones from nearby riverbeds.

## TECHNICAL SPECS

- Adobe bricks were made of sand, clay, and water mixed with straw. The mixture was shaped using frames and dried in the sun.
- The Anasazi are known as the "basketmakers" because they used baskets to cook in instead of clay or metal cooking pots.
- At Chaco Canyon, the "great house" at Pueblo Bonito had as many as 800 rooms.
- At Mesa Verde, some ancient sites are high on cliffs. The Anasazi probably climbed to them using rope ladders or footholds carved into the rock.

The Cliff Palace at Mesa Verde is sheltered beneath an overhang. The round structures are ceremonial rooms named kivas.

# PUEBLO BUILDING

Peoples in the Americas built their homes with materials that were easily available. In the lowlands of Mesoamerica and the deserts of the Southwest, it rarely rains. Mud brick, or adobe, was the main building material. The Aztec and Maya used stone for public buildings such as temples and palaces.

Taos Pueblo, New Mexico, was built by the Taos people over 1,000 years ago. It has been lived in ever since.

## HOW TO...

Pueblo Bonito was the largest settlement in Chaco Canyon, New Mexico. It was built in a large D-shape, with its curved back facing the canyon wall, and could only be entered by ladder. It contained at least 800 joined rooms, built on several levels. It probably housed as many as 1,200 people at its height in the 12th century C.E.

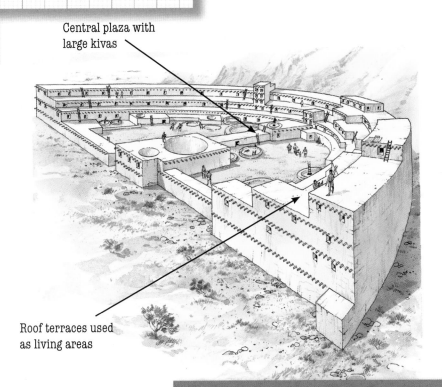

Central plaza with large kivas

Roof terraces used as living areas

The Aztec built single-story homes using adobe bricks made from sun-dried mud and straw. The houses had one big room with a roof of thatched straw.

## PUEBLO PEOPLES

To the north, the Pueblo peoples were influenced by techniques from Mexico. The Anasazi built "great houses," or large communal structures that each held many dwellings. The largest housed thousands of people. Access was by a system of ladders that led to doorways on the flat roofs. Circular pits named kivas, which were dug into the ground, were used for religious ceremonies.

## TECHNICAL SPECS

- The Aztec wove reed mats to sleep on the floor and built reed chests for clothes. The Inca had no furniture.
- The Maya made plaster to line their pueblo homes by burning limestone for 36 hours to make a powder. The powder was mixed with water to make plaster.
- Pueblo Bonito's original gateway was narrowed and then blocked completely.
- The lower rooms in the pueblo had no windows. They were probably used for storage.

# TENOCHTITLÁN

When the Spanish conquerors first saw the Aztec capital of Tenochtitlán in 1519 c.e. they could not believe their eyes. The city was far more sophisticated and larger than any European city. The city was laid out in a grid pattern. It had been built on swampy islands on Lake Texcoco in the Valley of Mexico.

This painting shows the ceremonial center of Tenochtitlán and the causeways linking it to the shores of Lake Texcoco.

Double temple pyramid

Rack to display heads of human sacrifices

## Center of Tenochtitlán

To build on the swampy land, the Aztecs created chinampas. These were built on reeds and mats weighted with stones and sunk between poles. On this base, the Aztec piled mud from the lake to form a *chinampa*, or mound.

## BUILDING ON AN ISLAND

The Aztec built two terracotta aqueducts to carry freshwater to the island. The island was accessed by three causeways. Only the center of the island was strong enough to support stone structures. This was where the main temples and palaces were located. Ordinary people lived in one-room, one-story adobe buildings.

## TECHNICAL SPECS

- The causeways had bridges in the middle that could be pulled up to defend the city.
- People used flat-bottomed canoes to travel around the city's canals.
- The Spaniards claimed that the causeways were wide enough for 10 horses to walk side by side.
- The Templo Mayor in the heart of the city was rebuilt seven times. Each temple was built on top of the last. Its weight made it sink into the mud of Lake Texcoco.
- Modern-day Mexico City is built on the foundations of Tenochtitlán.
- The Aztec used human waste from public toilets to fertilize crops.

# NAZCA LINES

The Nazca culture flourished in southern Peru between 100 B.C.E. and 800 C.E. The Nazca are best known for the massive drawings they made on the stony surface of the Nazca desert. The purpose of these drawings remains a mystery. The Nazca were also skilled potters and textile makers.

This design is known as the hummingbird. Other images show familiar animals such as a whale and a monkey.

## HOW TO...

The Nazca Lines cover an area of 190 square miles (500 sq km); the longest is over 5 miles (8 km) long. Some align with the setting sun on important days such as the winter solstice, the shortest day of the year (December 21). The builders may have plotted the lines from nearby hills, as the shapes are impossible to make out from the desert floor.

Line aligns with the setting sun

Darker rocks pushed to the side

## MYSTERIOUS LINES

The huge drawings the Nazca created in the desert show geometric shapes and lines, but also animals, birds, flowers, and trees. The lines were made by removing the reddish pebbles from the desert floor to uncover the whitish ground beneath. The lines have been preserved for centuries in the dry conditions. They may have been planned by studying the ground from low foothills nearby. Their purpose remains a mystery after many centuries. Some people have even claimed that they were intended to guide aliens in spaceships.

## TECHNICAL SPECS

- The Nazca Lines cover 190 square miles (500 sq km) of the Nazca desert, which is one of the driest places in the world.
- Creating the lines exposed a sublayer of soil that contains high levels of lime. The lime hardened in the sun's heat, helping to preserve the lines.
- The largest shape is 660 feet (200 m) across. For centuries it was thought the shapes could only be seen from the air, but in fact they can be seen clearly from the nearby hilltops.
- The Nazca Lines were probably carved using simple tools like wooden stakes.

# TRANSPORTATION

Reed boats known as balsa are still used on Lake Titicaca, in the highlands of modern-day Bolivia.

Unlike other ancient cultures, the Aztec, Inca, and Maya did not develop a wheel for transportation. Wheeled vehicles would have been of limited use in the mountains or forests. Neither did they have horses for riding. Most journeys were made on foot or by boat, especially across lakes or around the coast.

The Maya and Aztec made canoes from hollowed-out tree trunks. In the Aztec capital, Tenochtitlán, the island city was crisscrossed by canals that were crowded with canoes. Families moored canoes in back of their homes.

## REED BOATS

Timber was in short supply, so boats were often made from reeds that grew around lakes. They were trimmed and bound into tight bundles that were tied together to form a boat. The reeds meant the boats were light and strong. They were shaped so that each end of the boat was curved to help it move through the water more easily. Another form of transportation was the llama. The Inca used the llama to carry loads up steep mountainsides.

## TECHNICAL SPECS

- Larger reed boats were up to 20 feet (6 m) long. They had wooden masts and reed sails.
- In 1947 the Norwegian Thor Heyerdahl crossed the Pacific Ocean in a reed raft based on Inca designs. He believed ancient South Americans traded with the islands of the South Pacific.
- The Aztec used wheels on toys, but not on vehicles.
- The Inca prized llamas so highly they did not eat them for meat.

Llamas were used by the Inca for carrying loads and for their wool, which was woven into clothes and blankets.

# INCA ROADS AND BRIDGES

The heart of the Inca Empire was the imperial city of Cusco. Every road led directly to Cusco. Oddly for a civilization that never used the wheel, the Inca still built a well-developed and extensive road system. They were master builders and used their skill to build roads up steep mountainsides and to put bridges across deep valleys.

Inca roads used shallow steps to climb up hillsides; on steeper slopes, the roads zigzagged back and forth.

Inca roads crossed deep ravines by suspension bridges made of cables of twisted plant fiber.

## COMMUNICATIONS NETWORK

The two main road systems ran from north to south. El Camino de la Costa ran along the Pacific Ocean for 2,500 miles (4,000 km). Inland, the Camino Real, or Royal Way, ran through the Andes from Ecuador south to Argentina, via Cusco. The two were linked by smaller roads. Messengers (*chasquis*) ran in relays with messages to and from Cusco. The Inca army also used the roads to march to the corners of the empire. Ordinary people were not allowed to use them. Where the terrain was interrupted by canyons, the Inca built rope suspension bridges.

## TECHNICAL SPECS

- The Camino Real was made from flat stones, while the coastal road was paved with clay bricks.
- The coastal road was up to 15 feet (5 m) wide. The mountain road was narrower. It followed the contours of the landscape.
- Royal messengers could cover 200 miles (320 km) a day.
- On steep mountainsides, roads zigzagged or went up stone steps.
- Branches were braided between cables to form a bridge. Two more cables acted as guardrails.
- The bridge across Apurimac Canyon on the Camino Real was 120 feet (36 m) above a river.

# ASTRONOMY

El Caracol at Chichén Itzá was used to study the heavens. It was aligned with the movements of Venus.

The Maya believed their gods lived in the sky. They based their own lives on interpreting what they saw in the sky. Their astronomers worked out the cycles of heavenly events. The Aztec and Inca were also eager astronomers. The sun and moon played an important role in their ceremonies and rituals.

The Maya used the cycles of the sun and moon to predict the future. Priests told rulers the best times for actions, such as going to war. The Maya also studied the planets, particularly Venus and Mars. They had the most advanced calendar of the ancient Americans.

## ALIGNMENT WITH THE SUN

Like the Maya, the Aztec aligned temples and pyramids with the summer and winter solstices. The Inca also worked out the time of the solstices. It helped them know when to plant crops.

## TECHNICAL SPECS

- The Aztec planned the chief pyramids in Tenochtitlán so the sun's rays passed between them on the spring equinox, March 21.
- The Maya worked out that a lunar month is 29.5302 days long. The precise length is 29.53059 days.
- The Maya could predict solar eclipses, but not where they would be visible.
- The Hitching Post of the Sun at Machu Picchu indicated the two equinoxes. The sun was directly above the stone pillar on March 21 and September 23, so it cast almost no shadow.

Machu Picchu was a sacred Inca city where priests performed ceremonies to keep the sun in its place.

# CALENDARS

The Mayan calendar is the most famous creation of the Maya. In December 2012, the Mayan calendar was headline news. People waited to see if the world would end on December 21, the end of a cycle of the Mayan calendar. The Aztec adopted the Mayan calendar, but gave the days and months Aztec names.

This Maya stone carving is a representation of the calendar used for "long counts."

In this carving of the solar calendar, the Mayan god of time is surrounded by the names of the months.

## COMPLEX CALENDARS

There were three Mayan calendars. The first was based on a sacred year of 260 days. It had two different simultaneous weeks: a numbered week of 13 days and a named week of 20 days. The second calendar was based on the solar year and was used by farmers. It had 18 months of 20 days, with five unlucky extra days to make a year of 365 days. A third calendar was used for "long counts" made up of cycles. The longest cycle was an "alautun" of 23,040,000,000 days. Both the Maya and Aztec feared the end of a cycle as an unlucky time.

## TECHNICAL SPECS

- The Maya believed that anyone born on one of the five unlucky days was cursed.
- The Mayan calendar began on August 13, 3114 B.C.E. No one knows why they chose that date.
- The Maya and Aztec thought cycles followed each other.
- The sacred calendar had two wheels, one with 13 numbers and the other with 20 named days. The wheels turned to match a number with a day. The whole cycle took 260 days.
- At the end of a cycle, the Aztec let all their fires go out. A sacrifice was killed and his heart removed. A priest lit a fire inside his empty chest that was used to relight all the other fires.

# WRITING

Individual knotted strings were tied onto a cord to create a complete record—but today no one knows how to read the strings.

The Maya and the Aztec both developed a system of writing using hieroglyph characters, a little similar to that of the ancient Egyptians. The characters were carved in stone or written in documents. They both devised counting systems that used base 20. The Inca never developed a writing system. They kept records using quipu, which were knotted strings.

Mayan writing had around 850 hieroglyphs. It was difficult to read. Each symbol stood for a word or part of a word, but could also stand for an idea or a sound. The Maya wrote on stone and in books called codices. The Aztec also used hieroglyphs, but few people could read. Both the Maya and the Aztec used symbols for numbers.

## INCA QUIPU

Inca quipu were knotted strings of various thicknesses and colors. The information recorded varied according to the type of knot, the color, and position of the strings.

## TECHNICAL SPECS

- The paper used in codices was made from the fibers of the maguey cactus plant. The folded pages were bound in animal skin.
- The Maya wrote in codices using fine brushes of animal hair. They kept ink in conch shells cut in half. Four codices still exist.
- Quipu were used to keep records of taxes, population numbers, and business deals.
- Quipu were created and read by trained accountants. Some quipu had more than 2,000 strings.
- To show something was further away, the Aztec drew a glyph closer to the top of a page.
- Mayan number symbols were arranged on three lines.

Mayan writing was carved into stone for sacred purposes and to record important dates and events.

# METALWORK

When the Spanish conquerors arrived in the Inca capital at Cusco, they could not believe their eyes. Gold and silver were everywhere. Ancient peoples in Peru started to make objects out of gold 3,000 years ago. The Moche of northern Peru were probably the first to cast metal, around 100 C.E.

Gold and silver were plentiful in Peru. Metals were collected by sifting river gravel in trays. Flecks of metal were easy to spot. The Inca also dug some shallow mines.

This gold figure was cast by Inca smiths as a handle for a knife used to sacrifice animals in religious rituals.

## SPREADING SKILLS

The Moche were skilled metalworkers. They cast objects by pouring molten metal into molds. The technique spread north, reaching Mesoamerica about 900 C.E.

## GOLD WORKERS

Goldsmiths were important members of Aztec society. They cast objects using the "lost wax" method. The Inca both cast gold and also used cold working. This involved beating the gold into thin sheets that could then be shaped and soldered together to form hollow objects.

## TECHNICAL SPECS

- The Moche developed a method of adding a thin layer of gold—gold plate—to copper. They dissolved gold in acid, then placed a copper object in the liquid. Gold coated the copper and was heated to make it bind permanently.
- The Inca called gold "the sweat of the sun" and silver "the tears of the moon."
- Inca and Mesoamerican smiths used gold, silver, and copper, with some tin, lead, and platinum. They did not use iron.
- The earliest known goldwork was made in Peru around 3,000 years ago.
- The Inca smelted metals in clay furnaces with holes in the front to allow a flow of air to raise the heat of the fire enough to melt metals.

This gold figurine was made by the Inca. In Cusco, the Inca "planted" gold and silver corn cobs in a garden.

# WEAPONS AND WARFARE

The Aztec, Inca, and Maya were warring peoples. Warriors were elite in their societies. These peoples expanded their territory by going to war against their neighbors. Another important reason to go to war was to capture prisoners for sacrifice to keep the gods happy.

All Mesoamerican males served in the army from the age of 17. Weapons were wooden clubs and spears

This clay model of a warrior was made around 600 C.E. by the Zapotec people who lived in Mexico.

This carving shows a Mayan warrior in a helmet decorated with feathers. Feathers were a symbol of high status.

## TECHNICAL SPECS

- Aztec warriors carried a wooden maquahuitl, or war club. It was 30 inches (76 cm) long and had grooved sides set with obsidian stone blades.
- The atlatl helped throw spears over 300 feet (90 m). It was a wooden shaft with a handle on one end and a cup on the other, into which the end of the spear fitted.
- Flint was used to make sharp knives.
- Despite being well trained and large, both the Inca and Aztec armies were easily defeated by a tiny number of Spaniards. The invaders had guns, steel swords, and horses, which the Inca and Aztec had never seen.

tipped with obsidian (Aztec) or bronze (Inca). The Inca used slingshots made from hide or wood to throw rocks. They also threw bolas, which were leather straps with rocks tied at the ends. When thrown at an enemy, they wrapped around his legs and tripped him up.

## ARMOR AND SHIELDS

Warriors wore quilted cotton tunics and wooden armor. Most shields and helmets were made from wood, but the Aztec made shields from jaguar skin and brightly colored tropical feathers.

# MEDICINE

This 20th-century painting shows Ixcuina, the Aztec goddess believed to look after women in childbirth.

In Mesoamerica and the Andes, people thought the gods made them sick if they did something to make them angry. But although healers called on the gods for help, they also understood a lot about how the human body worked. They used medicinal plants to cure different ailments. Cures were a mixture of magic, offerings to please the gods, and practical medicine.

The Aztec and the Inca performed surgery with knives made from flint or obsidian. They stitched wounds with human hair or vegetable fibers, using needles made from bone. Inca surgeons bored holes in skulls to relieve headaches and could amputate limbs if necessary.

## REMEDIES AND PREVENTION

The Aztec used plants as remedies. They thought tobacco cleared the head and the coca plant deadened pain. They grew medicinal plants in special botanical gardens. The Aztec took good care of their mouths. After eating, they rinsed their mouths with water and used thorns as toothpicks.

## TECHNICAL SPECS

- Broken limbs were mended by joining the broken ends of a bone together. A mixture of plant root was applied, and the limb was held in place by wooden splints bound with cords.
- Tartar was removed from teeth with charcoal and saltwater, or a mixture of alum, salt, chili, and cochineal.
- The Inca chewed coca leaves to help combat altitude sickness.
- Quinine comes from a Peruvian tree. Ancient peoples used it to prevent and treat malaria; it is used for the same purpose today.
- The Spaniards brought smallpox. Native peoples had no immunity, so the disease killed millions.

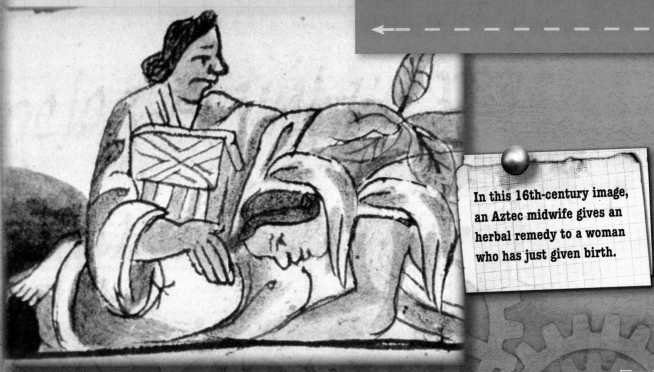

In this 16th-century image, an Aztec midwife gives an herbal remedy to a woman who has just given birth.

# TEXTILES

Some of the most remarkable textiles in South America were some of the earliest. The Paracas people, who lived in the Andes from about 900 B.C.E. to 400 C.E., wove elaborate designs into their cloth. For the Inca who followed them, textiles were their most valuable possessions. They were more valuable than gold.

A descendant of the Inca weaves a colorful textile on a backstrap loom. The long threads are the warp threads.

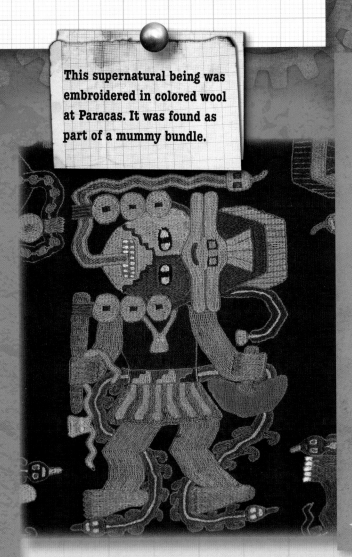

This supernatural being was embroidered in colored wool at Paracas. It was found as part of a mummy bundle.

## TECHNICAL SPECS

- In Paracas, cloth was dyed with bright colors such as indigo (blue) and pink.
- Paracas cloth was often heavily embroidered. It was used to wrap dead bodies before they were buried.
- One ancient Peruvian noble was buried with 300 pounds (135 kg) of cotton in his grave.
- Cochineal beetles, which live on cactus plants, were used for red dye. To make 1 pound (454 g) of dye it took 70,000 beetles.
- Llamas and alpacas produced a glossy wool, but the finest wool came from their relative, the wild vicuña.

The Paracas people wove textiles from the wool of llamas and alpacas and from plant fibers, such as cotton. Designs woven into the cloth helped to preserve the tribe's religious beliefs. Some textiles are up to 115 feet (35 m) long: to produce them would have required many workers.

## BACKSTRAP LOOM

Andean peoples wove on a backstrap loom. One end of the warp threads was attached to a wooden bar that was hung on a tree or post. The other end was strapped around the weaver's back. The weaver altered the tautness of the yarn by leaning back as she passed the weft thread through the warp threads.

# POTTERY

**The Mesoamericans and Inca were skilled potters, but they did not use potter's wheels or kilns. Every vessel was shaped by hand. The pots were richly decorated using a variety of techniques. The best ceramics were used for religious ceremonies or by the rich.**

Pottery in both the Andes and Mesoamerica was made by shaping coils of clay, by molding the clay, or by carving blocks of clay. Mesoamerican potters often produced slipware. Before a pot was fired, it was decorated with semiliquid clay, known as slip. Different colored slips were used to paint decoration on the pot. Instead of using kilns,

The Moche made "portrait vessels," which showed people or gods. Other designs showed animals.

Mimbres potters crushed plants and rocks to make paint. They made brushes from feathers and twigs.

early American potters fired their pots in an open fire. They made pottery known as blackware by controlling how much oxygen the pot received as it was fired.

## DISTINCTIVE POTTERY

Some of the most distinctive pottery was made by the Moche of northern Peru. They made pots in complex human and animal forms. The pots had U-shaped "stirrup" spouts. From the ninth century C.E., the Mogollon people of Arizona and New Mexico produced a distinctive black-on-white pottery, known as Mimbres. It is notable for the distinctive decoration featuring elaborate geometric designs.

## TECHNICAL SPECS

- The Inca used molds to make basic pots such as the aryballos jar. It had a conical base, a tall flared neck, and handles on the sides.
- Most Inca pottery was polished red, with geometric patterns in red, white, and black.
- Whistling water jars were double vessels connected by hollow tubes. As water flowed from one vessel, it pushed air out of the other through a whistle. Some whistling jars were made in the shape of the quetzal, a bird sacred to both the Aztec and the Maya.
- The Maya covered their pots with a colored plaster called stucco.
- Mimbres pots were often buried with the dead. The pots were first "killed" by having a hole punched through their base.

# TIMELINE

**B.C.E.**

**3114** The Maya calendar begins on August 13.

**c.3000** Pottery is first made in the Americas, in what are now Colombia and Ecuador.

**c.1200** The Olmec culture appears in Mexico.

**c.900** The Olmec build the first pyramid in America, at La Venta.

**c.800** The Paracas culture appears in Peru; it is famed for its textiles.

**c.300** The earliest stages of Mayan culture appear in Mesoamerica.

**c.300** An unknown people begins building the great city of Teotihuacán in central Mexico.

**c.100** The Paracas culture disappears.

**C.E.**

**c.100** The Olmec culture in Mexico declines.

**c.100** The Moche of northern Peru begin to cast objects in metal.

**c.400** The Nazca of Peru begin drawing huge designs in the desert.

**c.500** The Maya build the city of Tikal, which has many tall pyramids.

**c.600** The Maya civilization reaches its height.

**c.600** Teotihuacán is abandoned for unknown reasons.

**c.600** Cahokia is founded in Illinois.

**c.850** The Maya civilization begins a decline.

**899** The Maya abandon the city of Tikal.

**c.900** The Pueblo build adobe communal dwellings in Chaco Canyon.

| | |
|---|---|
| **c.900** | Casting techniques reach Mesoamerica. |
| **c.1000** | The Mogollon culture reaches its classic phase, producing distinctive black-and-white Mimbres pottery. |
| **c.1070** | The Natchez people build Serpent Mound in Ohio. |
| **c.1100** | The Toltec emerge in Mexico, building a capital at Tula. |
| **c.1100** | At its peak, Cahokia in Illinois has 100 mounds. |
| **c.1100** | The Anasazi build cliff homes at Mesa Verde and Canyon de Chelly. |
| **c.1200** | The Aztec move into central Mexico from an origin farther to the north. |
| **c.1200** | The first Inca emperor, Manco Cápac, founds an empire from Cusco in the Andes. |
| **1325** | The Aztec begin their rise to power and build their capital Tenochtitlán in the middle of a shallow lake. |
| **1438** | The Inca build the sacred city of Machu Picchu in a remote mountaintop location. |
| **c.1470** | The Inca conquer the neighboring Chimu culture. |
| **1492** | Christopher Columbus crosses the Atlantic and lands on the island of Hispaniola in the Caribbean, marking European contact with the Americas. |
| **1498** | Columbus lands on mainland America. |
| **1517** | The first Spaniards land in Mexico, on the Yucatán Peninsula. They introduce illnesses, such as smallpox, to which native peoples have no immunity; within a century, these diseases devastate the population of Mesoamerica. |
| **1519** | Hernán Cortés lands in Mexico and begins to conquer the Aztec Empire. |
| **1521** | Cortés destroys the Aztec capital at Tenochtitlán; it will be rebuilt as Mexico City. |

# GLOSSARY

**canal**  An artificial waterway.

**cast**  To make objects by pouring molten metal into a mold.

**causeway**  A raised roadway across a lake or marsh.

**chinampa**  An artificial island built in a shallow lake for use as a "floating garden."

**codices**  (sing. codex) Early forms of books, with pages sewn together.

**embroider**  To sew a design onto a piece of cloth with colored thread.

**empire**  A large territory ruled by an emperor or empress.

**furnace**  A very hot oven used to fire clay or to melt metals.

**hieroglyph**  A picture or symbol used for writing. Hieroglyphs can stand for things or sounds, or both.

**irrigation**  Artificially watering fields in order to grow crops.

**kiln**  An oven used to harden pottery or bake bricks.

**"lost wax" method**  A way of making metal objects in which a wax model of the finished object is enclosed in a clay mold. When molten metal is poured in, the wax runs out, leaving the metal to cool and harden.

**Mesoamerica**  An area inhabited by similar cultures that included parts of modern-day Mexico, Guatemala, Honduras, Belize, El Salvador, and Nicaragua.

**pueblo**  A communal building made of adobe in the U.S. Southwest; the term is also used to describe the peoples who built them.

**pyramid**  A four-sided structure that tapers to a point.

**slip**  A layer of liquid clay used to decorate pottery.

**staple**  A food that makes up the major part of a diet.

**terrace**  A flat bank of earth with steep sides.

**ziggurat**  A pyramid that rises in steps to a flat top.

# FURTHER INFORMATION

## BOOKS

Baquedano, Elizabeth. *Aztec, Inca, and Maya* (Eyewitness Books). DK Publishing, 2011.

Bell-Rehwoldt, Sheri. *Amazing Maya Inventions You Can Build Yourself* (Build It Yourself). Nomad Press, 2007.

Croy, Anita. *Ancient Pueblo* (National Geographic Investigates). National Geographic Children's Books, 2007.

Heinrichs, Ann. *The Aztecs* (Technology of the Ancients). Marshall Cavendish Children's Books, 2011.

Malam, John, and Fiona MacDonald. *100 Things You Should Know About Pyramids*. Mason Crest, 2009.

Snedden, Robert. *Aztec, Inca, and Maya* (Technology in Times Past). Saunders Book Co., 2011.

## WEBSITES

www.civilization.ca/maya/
Canadian Museum of Civilization information about the Maya.

www.ancientworlds.net/aw/
Article/729894
Ancientworlds.com guide to Inca technology, with links.

www.britishmuseum.org/explore/
cultures/the_americas/
aztecs_mexica.aspx
British Museum introduction to the culture of the Aztec.

# INDEX